# PICTURES
# OF MOTION
# AND
# PICTURES
# THAT MOVE

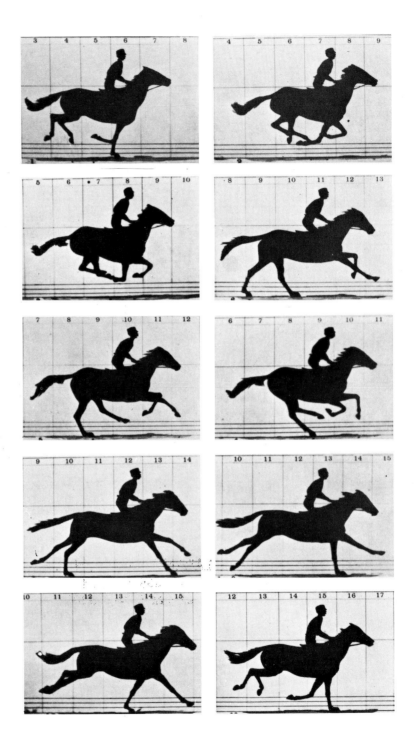

# PICTURES OF MOTION AND PICTURES THAT MOVE

Eadweard Muybridge
and the
Photography of Motion

## STEPHEN MANES

Coward, McCann & Geoghegan, Inc.

New York

*For Mom and Dad*

*Photo Credits*

Frontispiece, pages 15, 29 (top), 33: Stanford University Archives; pages 3, 23: reprinted by permission of the University of California Press, copyright 1975 by the Regents of the University of California; pages 4, 27, 32, 34, 37, 38, 47: Heritage Unit, Museum & Art Gallery, Fairfield West, Kingston Upon Thames; page 6: the California Historical Society; pages 8, 9, 10 (top), 11, 12, 13, 21, 22: courtesy, the Bancroft Library, the University of California, Berkeley; pages 10 (bottom), 29 (bottom): Division of Photographic History, Smithsonian Institution; pages 17, 28, 30–31: Stanford Family Collection. Stanford University Museum of Art; page 24: Collection, the Museum of Modern Art; pages 25, 42: reproduced from the Collections of the Library of Congress; page 35: Stanford University Museum of Art, Muybridge Collection; page 41: gift of Jane Lathrop Stanford. Stanford University Museum of Art 12038; pages 48–49, 50, 51, 53, 54: New York Public Library, Division of Art, Prints & Photographs.

First printing

Designed by Charlotte Staub

*Printed in the United States of America*

LIBRARY OF CONGRESS CATALOGING IN PUBLICATION DATA

Manes, Stephen.
  Pictures of motion and pictures that move.

  Bibliography: p.
  Includes index.
  Summary: A biography of the photographer and motion-picture pioneer whose early efforts at photographing motion included proving that at one period of its stride, a running horse has all four feet off the ground.
  1. Muybridge, Eadweard, 1830–1904—Juvenile literature. 2. Cinematographers—United States—Biography—Juvenile literature. [1. Muybridge, Eadweard, 1830–1904.    2. Photographers.    3. Cinematography—History]    I. Title.
TR849.M87M36    770.924  [B]  [92]    81–15292
ISBN 0–698–20550–2    AACR2

# CONTENTS

# PICTURES
# OF MOTION
# AND
# PICTURES
# THAT MOVE

# 1. FROM MUGGERIDGE TO MUYBRIDGE

S peed!

Motion!

Railroad baron Leland Stanford had built his enormous fortune on them. In 1869, as president of the Central Pacific Railroad, he himself had driven the famous "golden spike"— the final link in the tracks that made coast-to-coast train travel possible in America for the very first time.

Soon another kind of speed and motion began to fascinate him. Following doctors' orders to get more sunshine and fresh air, Stanford began visiting racetracks. In no time at all, the massive millionaire became an absolute fanatic about horses.

Leland Stanford was one of California's biggest boosters. He'd been governor between 1862 and 1864; people still addressed him by his old title. His newest scheme was to bring his beloved state an international reputation in racing. He

Eadweard Muybridge (then Muygridge) at about age thirty. The earliest photograph of him known to exist.

hoped to develop a stable of horses that could outrun the best in the world. And he intended to use scientific study to help him do it.

Stanford believed the key to success in breeding and training racehorses was to learn precisely how the animals moved. That was easier said than done. The human eye and brain were by far the best tools then available for the study of motion. Even the sharpest observers disagreed about what they saw in horses' swift, complex movements. In one experiment, Stanford and his friends ran a horse over a smooth, sandy track so they could study the well-defined footprints afterward. It was a good try, but the results led to more argument than enlightenment.

No question was more hotly debated than whether a swiftly   3

Leland Stanford:
railroad baron, politician,
and horse fancier.

trotting horse actually has all four feet off the ground at once
for some brief instant. Stanford and many others thought so.

"Preposterous!" their detractors blustered. "Impossible! The
horse could not support itself! Flying horses exist only in
myths!"

But the Governor kept insisting he was right, and the argument raged on. A rumor soon spread that Stanford and an
Eastern newspaper editor had bet $25,000 on the issue. The
purse would go to the one who could prove his point about
4 "unsupported transit" once and for all.

The rumor may have been entirely untrue, but it swept across the country. It was still going around when one of Leland Stanford's friends suggested that a photographer named Eadweard Muybridge (ED-wurd MY-bridge) might be just the man to settle the dispute.

It had taken Eadweard Muybridge a good many years to become one of the American West's best-known photographers. In fact, it had taken him a good many years to become Eadweard Muybridge. Born in Kingston-on-Thames, England, in 1830, he was originally named Edward James Muggeridge.

But at the age of twenty-one, the young Englishman set sail for the United States. For his new start in a new land, he gave himself a new name—but a very old one. In the town of his birth there stood a monument called the "Coronation Stone." According to local legend, seven Saxon kings had been crowned on it long ago. Two of those kings had been named "Eadweard"; it said so right on the monument. So Edward Muggeridge adopted the kingly spelling: if it was good enough for royalty, it would certainly do for him. No one knows exactly why, but he also took to calling himself "Muygridge." When he arrived in America, he found that the natives usually misspelled both his new names. With the stubbornness he was to display throughout his life, he hung onto them anyway.

In his first few years in the New World, Muygridge did plenty of traveling. As an agent for British publishers, he roamed throughout the East and South selling books to bookshops. But after a few years, he caught the "western fever" that seemed to be infecting the country. Muygridge moved his business to San Francisco, where a friend named Silas Selleck had opened a photography studio.

The California Gold Rush was over, but San Francisco was still full of western wildness—right down to cold-blooded shootings on the streets and vigilante hangings afterward. As a bookseller, Muygridge offered the city a much-needed dose of culture. He quickly became a respected citizen.

5

A flyer advertising Muygridge's book business, about 1858.

In 1860, Muygridge left his flourishing bookshop in his brother's care and set out on a journey back to England. The Overland Stage was his choice for the first leg of the trip. At best, this new stagecoach service was bone-rattling and uncomfortable. Muygridge had the misfortune to try it at its worst.

Heading down a hill in northeast Texas, the stagecoach driver lost control of his horses. The brakes failed, and the coach ran wild. When it crashed into trees and broke up, two passengers were killed.

Thrown out the rear, Muygridge was badly injured. When he regained consciousness, he could neither hear, taste, smell, nor see properly. After a long convalescence, he finally finished his journey to England. There doctors prescribed two of the best medicines then available: fresh air and exercise.

While civil war raged across the Atlantic, Muygridge kept himself busy in England. He invented and patented a washing machine and a printing device, neither of which anyone seems to have used. But in keeping with doctors' orders, he also learned a new trade—one he could practice outdoors. When he returned to a more civilized San Francisco in 1867, he no longer sold books. Instead, he set up shop as a photographer.

He also made another change, one that would last for the rest of his life: he had become Eadweard Muy*b*ridge. Except behind the camera. With his love of unusual names, he signed his photos "Helios," after the Greek god of the sun.

In San Francisco, Muybridge shared his friend Selleck's photographic salon. But while Selleck stuck to the indoor comfort of portraiture, "Helios" stuck to his doctors' orders. Muybridge ranged far and wide in his "flying studio"—a horse-drawn darkroom on wheels.

Luck was running Muybridge's way again. Outdoor scenes were in great demand, for a device called the stereoscope had become a craze. In parlors throughout America, people were passing their stereoscope viewers around and marveling at everything from pyramids to palaces.

What made the stereoscope (STAIR-ee-uh-skoap) so special? The same thing that made "3-D" movies a fad nearly a hun- 7

Muybridge's "Flying Studio" on a San Francisco street. About 1870. A bit of self-promotion in a photo of the ornate Savings and Loan Society building. Half of a stereograph.

dred years later: a lifelike illusion of depth. Humans sense depth because each of their two eyes sees the world from a slightly different angle. A regular photograph seems flat because it's taken from only one angle with one "eye"—the camera lens.

But the stereoscope was different. The camera used for stereo photos was actually *two* cameras placed side by side. The two lenses were set about as far apart as two human eyes and captured two nearly identical pictures from two slightly different angles. The two photographs were mounted on a card and then placed in a viewer. The person looking through the viewer saw a different picture through each eye; the brain blended them to give a realistic illusion of depth.

8

San Francisco "by moonlight." 1869. Muybridge may have taken this picture in the daytime and used photographic trickery to give it a moonlight effect. Half of a stereograph.

But not absolutely realistic. Like all photographs for many years to come, stereographs were in black and white. That didn't seem to bother an eager public. Travelers gobbled up souvenir stereoscope pictures of the sights they'd seen; less fortunate souls ordered photos of people and places they knew they'd never be able to visit. Eadweard Muybridge supplied stereoscope pictures to help satisfy the enormous curiosity about the American West.

Like most photographers, Muybridge had to master his craft on the job. Taking pictures was hard work—not just a matter of pushing a button and letting someone else do the rest. In his day, negatives were made on heavy glass plates much like windowpanes. First the photographer had to coat the plate in  9

The steamer *Active,* 1868. Taken during Muybridge's voyage to Alaska, this was one of his early efforts at photographing a moving subject. Full stereograph.

A table-model stereoscope (in glass case) surrounded by a display of stereographs. Hand-held stereoscopes looked much like this one, but with a short handle instead of a candlestick base.

301. North Point Dock

Muybridge at North Point Dock, San Francisco, about 1867.

darkness with a solution of light-sensitive chemicals he had prepared. Then he had to take the picture while the plate was still wet. Next he had to develop it right away in darkness to bring out the image, "fix" it with more chemicals to set the image, and finally wash and dry it. As Muybridge wrote years later, "All this involved a vast amount of tedious and careful manipulation."

Even in an indoor studio, this "wet plate" process could be tricky, but out in the field it tried the patience of the most experienced roving cameramen. The messy, smelly chemicals were bad enough, but the photographer also had to drag along bulky cameras and lenses, heavy plates, and a portable darkroom. If a picture didn't turn out, he could wash the plate and 11

*59 Yosemite Hotel (same as Stereo 24*

The Yosemite Hotel, Yosemite Valley, California, 1867. One of Muybridge's many Yosemite scenes.

480 Fort Wrangle from Rock Cod

Natives in Alaska, 1868.

reuse it, but if a plate broke, it meant one less picture he could bring back. And if his chemicals spilled or leaked away, all he could do was return home, get more, and start over.

Yet Muybridge thrived on these difficulties. After photographing everything worth looking at in San Francisco, he roamed elsewhere. On mule and mustang, he carried his burdensome equipment up hills and down canyons to remote viewpoints in the Yosemite Valley. Often he'd arrive just after dawn and wait patiently for hours until the sun lit the scene exactly as he wanted it.

His reputation grew. The United States Army hired him to sail to Alaska and bring back views of America's newest territory. Closer to home, he photographed ships, geysers, islands, railroads, lighthouses, and the aftermath of an earthquake. He went back to Yosemite and took huge pictures that won prizes in European exhibitions. And he even found a few spare moments to court and marry Flora Shallcross Stone, a divorced woman half his age.

13

# 2. TO FREEZE A MOVING HORSE

In 1872, when Leland Stanford and Eadweard Muybridge met for the first time, nobody could have guessed what extraordinary things that meeting would lead to. Nobody ever wrote down exactly what was said that day, or exactly what happened in the days immediately following. But things seem to have gone something like this:

Eadweard Muybridge was standing impatiently in Leland Stanford's posh Sacramento parlor wishing the Governor would get down to business. Business, Muybridge assumed, would be a commission for some photographs: portraits of the Governor's family, perhaps, or pictures of one of his lavish houses. But Stanford was a slow, ponderous speaker, and he kept droning on and on about horses.

The photographer's restless eyes drifted to the thick carpets,

The parlor of Leland Stanford's house at Sacramento, 1872.

the golden picture frames, the ornate chandelier. He scratched his long gray beard, hoping the Governor would get to the point. But £eland $tanford (as one local writer enjoyed spelling his name) was not someone to be interrupted.

"Mr. Muybridge," Stanford concluded at last, "I want you to photograph my horse, Occident."

Muybridge nodded with relief. So that was the job! Now everything made sense. Occident was famous. Once a lowly cart horse, he had been trained according to Stanford's philosophies and was challenging the fastest trotters in the West. Of course the Governor would want pictures of him.

But Stanford hadn't quite finished. "I want you to photograph him trotting past the camera at a pace of two minutes and thirty seconds," he added.

Muybridge stopped nodding. Two minutes and thirty sec- 15

onds per mile? That was a pace of nearly twenty-five miles an hour! As far as he knew, no one had ever photographed *anything* moving that fast. Why, sharp pictures of people strolling were considered remarkable!

"Do you accept my proposal?" demanded Leland Stanford. "Can you do it?"

Muybridge thought it over. He enjoyed new photographic challenges, and this was certainly the biggest one yet. He weighed his words carefully, to avoid giving his new patron false hopes. "It may prove impossible, sir," he said. "But I'll certainly try."

"Excellent!" Stanford boomed. "Oh, and one thing more. I would like the picture to show the moment when all four of the horse's legs are clear of the ground."

Muybridge wondered if Leland Stanford had taken leave of his senses. Obviously the Governor did not know the first thing about photography. But Muybridge tried not to show his doubts. He was confident that if anybody could capture Occident in "flight," he would be the one to do it.

Muybridge had photographed waterfalls in Yosemite and had taken pictures from a moving ship in Alaska, so he was well aware of the problems he faced. Normally, once a plate was in his camera, he would take a picture simply by removing the lens cap, counting slowly to three or six or ten (depending on the light), and covering the lens again. Obviously, this wouldn't do for a running horse: it would streak past the lens and appear as a blur—if that. Muybridge knew he would have to cover and uncover his lens much more quickly than usual if he was going to capture the moving animal's image.

But with shorter exposures, light would become a problem. If enough didn't reach the plate, there would be no picture at all. He suspected that even his best lenses, ones with exceptional light-gathering ability, might not be able to do the job.

Leland Stanford and his horse-fancying cronies watched with great interest as Muybridge set up his camera at Sacramento's Union Park racecourse a few days later. "At least the day is clear," the photographer observed optimistically. But bright as

16

Two of Leland Stanford's horses at the Sacramento race track. In order to be photographed, the animals had to stand absolutely still.

the sun was, Muybridge knew he would need to take special steps to capture every possible ray.

With Stanford's approval—this was beginning to get expensive—Muybridge ordered the stablehands to round up every white sheet they could find. Then he got them to string up the sheets along the inside of the track so they would reflect light toward the camera—and serve as a contrasting background for the dark brown horse. Next, Occident was trained to run between the camera and the sheets without flinching.

At last everything was ready. Muybridge prepared a plate, loaded it in his camera, and waved his arm in the air. The driver goaded Occident down the track. As the horse passed by, 17

Muybridge quickly popped the cover off and on the lens. Then he returned to his dark tent and developed the plate. Stanford and his colleagues waited impatiently.

"Gentlemen," Muybridge told them when he finally emerged into the sunlight, "I have not yet succeeded." He had to repeat that theme all afternoon. At the camera he manipulated the lens cap faster and faster, then tried using his hat to cover and uncover the lens still more quickly, but each time he developed a photo, he discovered he had captured nothing at all.

The day's efforts weren't entirely worthless, though. They had taught Muybridge exactly what he would have to do to make this experiment succeed.

First, he would have to increase the sensitivity of his plates so that they would require less light to register an image. Though he had little need to do it in his everyday work, Muybridge knew how to accomplish this by adjusting the mixtures of chemicals he used in sensitizing and developing.

Muybridge also knew he would need a mechanical shutter to cover and uncover the lens faster than he could by hand. Today's cameras all have shutters built in, ready to open and close at the touch of a button. In Muybridge's time, shutters were never built into cameras, and few photographers used them at all; the hand and lens cap normally worked just fine. But the imaginative Muybridge had already invented and patented a shutterlike device he called a "Sky Shade." He used it to block out the sky during long exposures and prevent it from becoming washed out in his pictures. Since he already knew something about shutters, he was able to rig up a makeshift one before returning to the track the next day.

The second session was almost as frustrating as the first. Again and again Muybridge triggered his shutter and disappeared into his dark tent. Again and again, he stepped out and announced his failure. By day's end the best he had come up with was a hazy blur that looked less like a horse than a smudge. But he knew he was making progress, and he decided to try one last time.

18      Muybridge set to work building a faster shutter. When

triggered, a spring mechanism would make two wooden slats slide past each other in opposite directions. Two openings, one in each slat, would swiftly cross each other in front of the lens and uncover it for a tiny fraction of a second.

When this shutter was ready, Muybridge set it in front of his camera at the racecourse and made some trial exposures. Then he had Occident brought to the track. But the photographer's first few attempts entirely failed to capture the horse's image.

After a long morning of frustration, Muybridge emerged from the dark tent with a plate in his hand and a hint of a smile on his face. Leland Stanford stared eagerly at the negative. What he saw was little more than a silhouette, and a fuzzy one at that, but it showed Occident frozen in midstride. The Governor was pleased.

But not satisfied. Muybridge had not yet captured the horse at the proper moment. The photographer went back to his camera and tried again, but the pictures that came out always showed at least one of the horse's hoofs touching the ground.

Muybridge began to think it might be hopeless. Stanford's theories about the horse's stride might even be downright wrong. But as he watched the image on his latest plate gradually develop in the dim light of the dark tent, Muybridge began to grow excited about what he saw. Hurriedly he drained the plate and poured new chemicals over it to fix the image.

He stepped outside and looked at the dripping negative in the sunlight. Then he handed the plate to Stanford.

The Governor broke into a broad smile. This image, too, was indistinct, but beyond all doubt it showed Occident with all four legs off the ground. Leland Stanford finally had proof that he was right about the "flying" horse.

Stanford congratulated Muybridge on a job well done. But that compliment, his own satisfaction, and a far from lavish fee were the only immediate rewards Muybridge received for accomplishing a singular photographic feat. If Leland Stanford had indeed made his famous bet, he certainly never shared the profits with the man who had won it for him.          19

# 3. MURDER

Back in San Francisco, Muybridge returned to business as usual. Ranging up the coast, he shot views of California wineries, Oregon scenery, and the aftermath of a bitter war between the United States Army and the Modoc Indians.

In 1874, while he was away on one such expedition, his wife Flora gave birth to a boy. The photographer loved names too much to give his son an ordinary one, but this time he outdid himself. The child was christened Floredo Helios Muybridge.

Soon afterward, Muybridge discovered that his wife had struck up a romance with a local dandy who called himself Major Harry Larkyns. After warning Larkyns to stay away from Flora, Muybridge learned the affair had been going on so long that Larkyns might possibly be Floredo's real father. The news shattered him. First disheartened, then enraged, Muybridge rushed to Calistoga, where Larkyns was working as a

Flora Shallcross Muybridge at Woodward's Gardens, San Francisco, 1870. Muybridge's signature, "Helios," appears at lower right on the grate.

surveyor for a mine. Arriving at a party at the mine superintendent's house, Muybridge asked to see Larkyns outside for a moment.

When his rival came out, Muybridge drew a pistol and stepped forward. "Good evening, Major," he said. "My name is Muybridge. Here is the answer to the message you sent my wife." Muybridge pulled the trigger. Larkyns staggered back and fell dead.

The photographer gave himself up at once. While lawyers prepared his case, he spent four unhappy months in jail. Then he went on trial for his life.

Although Muybridge insisted he had known exactly what he was doing when he shot Harry Larkyns, his attorneys entered a plea of not guilty by reason of insanity. In the courtroom, the photographer heard friends and associates testify to

21

Muybridge in Yosemite, 1872. He is sitting on a heavy photographic equipment box.

Muybridge at Contemplation Rock, Glacier Point, Yosemite Valley, California, 1872. At Muybridge's murder trial, this picture was cited as evidence of his insanity.

his excitability and eccentricity. One colleague claimed that no sane man would photograph himself standing at the edge of a sheer cliff—as Muybridge had. "And certainly," the witness went on, "no sane photographer would refuse to take a picture merely because it didn't suit his taste"—something the selective Muybridge did all the time.

But none of the testimony managed to convince the jury that the defendant was really insane. Instead, in keeping with the Wild West's tradition of defending and avenging one's honor, they decided Muybridge had been justified in committing murder. They found the defendant not guilty.　　23

When Eadweard Muybridge heard those words in the court-room, a flood of emotion engulfed him. He sobbed uncontrollably, and for many minutes he could not speak. After four months in prison, he had begun to lose hope. Now he was once more a free man.

Though out of prison, Muybridge was by no means out of trouble. With his reputation compromised, his career interrupted, and his wife suing him for divorce and alimony, he thought it best to leave the country for a while. He arranged a photographic expedition in Central America. While he was gone, Flora Muybridge fell ill and died.

Muybridge came back to San Francisco, placed his son in an orphanage, and tried to resume the life he had led before the murder. His most successful new work was a panorama of San Francisco taken from Nob Hill. Using eleven eight-by-ten-inch plates and "panning," or turning, the camera so that each suc-

The title page of Muybridge's Central America album. A small sampling of the photographs he brought back from his 1875–1876 journey.

**PANORAMA OF SAN FRANCISCO**

CALIFORNIA-STREET HILL.

KEY.

MUYBRIDGE,
LANDSCAPE, MARINE, ARCHITECTURAL, AND ENGINEERING
PHOTOGRAPHER.

Muybridge's classic panorama of San Francisco, 1877. Note the claim in the text at center: "Horses photographed while running or trotting at full speed."

cessive photo began where the last one left off, Muybridge put together a seven-foot-long, three-hundred-sixty-degree view of virtually every feature of the city. It proved so popular that he repeated it in a truly gigantic edition seventeen feet long.

With typical inventiveness, Muybridge boldly proposed that the county of Santa Clara hire him to make photographic copies to preserve its public records. The town fathers admired Muybridge's proposal—a forerunner of the microfilming systems in use today. They admitted it would be cheaper than copying the records by hand. But they rejected it nonetheless, claiming it would cost them too much money "in one lump."

So Eadweard Muybridge just went on taking pictures. And once again, the most important were to be the ones he would take for Leland Stanford.

25

# 4. THE HORSE TAKES THE PICTURES

Over the years, Leland Stanford had become more horse-mad than ever. He had purchased an enormous tract of land in Palo Alto, and he was transforming it into a huge horse farm, with his newest, fanciest mansion right on the grounds. No longer would the Governor's prize racehorses have to train with the riffraff at Sacramento. Now they had stables and tracks of their very own.

Questions about animal locomotion—the way animals move—continued to gnaw at the Governor. He still believed photography might help provide the answers. Once more he turned to Eadweard Muybridge.

With his additional experience and improved equipment, Muybridge now found it far easier to capture Occident in motion. This time he and Stanford decided to release the results of their work to the public. Unfortunately, the picture he and

An enlargement of one frame of Muybridge's Palo Alto studies. From *The Attitudes of Animals in Motion*, 1881.

Stanford published brought them as much criticism as fame.

Photographers of the time commonly retouched their photos—altering them for artistic effect. Often it was just a matter of painting out a wart or blemish in a portrait; sometimes picturesque clouds would be added to a landscape taken on a cloudless day. But sharp-eyed observers noticed that Muybridge's picture of Occident seemed to be more like a painting than a photograph.

And they happened to be right. Because he felt his original photo wasn't detailed enough for public display, Muybridge had an assistant paint a lifelike picture from it. Then Muybridge simply photographed the painting. The San Francisco Industrial Exhibition awarded the photo a medal, but critics called it a hoax. Could Muybridge really photograph a running horse, they asked, or could he not?

27

Leland Stanford knew the answer. Delighted with the latest photo of Occident, he decided to embark on a far grander project. He asked Muybridge to do no less than photograph his horses at every stage of their various strides. Money would be no object.

Muybridge eagerly moved to the Palo Alto farm to supervise these new experiments. Instead of one camera, he decided to use twelve in a row. That way, he would get a series of pictures showing the horse at twelve successive instants in its gait. Instead of trying to fire each of the twelve shutters at the precise instant the horse passed before it, Muybridge came up with a clever way to let the horse trigger the shutters as it ran by. In effect, the horse would take its own pictures!

Muybridge wasted no time spending Stanford's money. From New York he ordered the finest cameras available. From England he imported superb and costly lenses. With the help of telegraph experts from Stanford's railroad, he devised special electrically triggered shutters, faster than any developed before.

Occident trotting at full speed, 1877. This controversial "retouched" picture is actually a photograph of a painting by Muybridge's assistant, John Koch.

28

Setting up at Palo Alto, about 1880. Twenty-four-camera shed at right; background wall at left. The four boxes on wooden stands at either end of the track housed cameras for taking diagonal views. Although this picture was taken during the later stage of the experiments, the early equipment was basically similar.

On the south side of the racecourse, where the light was best, Muybridge's workmen built a darkroom and camera shed along the outside of the track. There they installed a dozen cameras and shutters in a row—one every twenty-one inches. On the inside of the track, they put up a long wooden fence for a backdrop. Then they covered it with white sheets marked with a black vertical line directly opposite each camera. Finally, they laid twelve pairs of electrical wires across the track and connected each pair to one of the shutters.

A patent office model of the shutter and background wall used at Palo Alto. Designed by telegraphers from Stanford's railroad, the electrical mechanism at the right of the shutter resembles a telegraph key.

One bright day in June of 1878, everything was ready. To prevent any charges of trickery, Stanford invited reporters and knowledgeable horsemen to witness Muybridge at work. As the crowd looked on, workers laid white powdered lime on the track to help reflect light upward. Stanford's chief trainer climbed into the sulky behind Abe Edgington and drove the fine trotter out from the stables. Muybridge and his assistants sensitized the plates and inserted them into the cameras.

Muybridge made his final preparations and held his arm high in the air. The crowd hushed. Then Muybridge dropped 29

A composite print from the first negatives to capture Abe Edgington in motion, 1878. The pictures at top right and bottom left clearly show all the horse's hooves off the ground at once.

his arm. The trainer cracked his whip, and Abe Edgington rushed down the track toward the cameras.

As the wheel of the sulky whizzed past, it pressed the first pair of wires on the ground together, then the second, the third, and so on. As each set of wires touched, it completed an electrical circuit, triggering the shutter of one camera. Then the next set of wires would complete a circuit and trigger the next shutter and then the next. It all happened so fast that the noisy shutters sounded like a drumroll.

30    Muybridge and his assistants disappeared into the darkroom.

While the guests waited expectantly, Stanford proudly showed them what his wealth had financed—expensive equipment that was unique in all the world. Twenty minutes later, Muybridge emerged from the darkroom carrying a plate.

There could be no more arguments. The glass negative clearly showed the horse, in silhouette, frozen at the beginning of his stride. And the pictures from the other cameras proved equally clear. Seen in proper sequence, they showed twelve phases of Abe Edgington's gait. The visitors were astonished.

And their hosts were overjoyed. For the first time anywhere, 31

Muybridge on horseback in front of the background wall at Palo Alto, 1878 (?).

Muybridge thought proudly, cameras had been used to separate a motion into a series of component parts. As for Leland Stanford, his dream had come true. He would finally be able to discover how his beloved horses really moved!

In the weeks that followed, Muybridge photographed the Governor's animals at every imaginable gait. They walked; they cantered; they trotted; they galloped. Day after day, the drumroll of the shutters echoed across the farm as wheels ran over wires. To get pictures of saddled horses, Muybridge strung fine silk threads across the track. As the horses ran into them, the threads stretched, triggered the shutters, and broke away harmlessly, all in a fraction of a second.

Once Muybridge had been content merely to devise ingenious ways of taking the pictures the Governor had asked for. Now he too found himself becoming fascinated with the way horses moved. He looked at paintings of the animals and found them

32

woefully inaccurate. He studied articles on the subject and discovered that many accepted ideas were simply wrong. Muybridge was no longer just a photographer. Like Stanford, he had become an eager student of animal locomotion.

That summer Muybridge gave public lectures on his work, illustrating them with slides of his photos. He especially enjoyed projecting his pictures beside paintings of moving horses. The comparison made the paintings look so absurd that the audience would often burst into laughter. To illustrate a horse's speed, most artists used the impossible "hobbyhorse" posture, with all four legs fully extended. In reality, as Muybridge's photos showed, a galloping horse has all his legs in the air only when they are gathered beneath his body. Muybridge tartly suggested artists should try to copy more from nature and less from other artists.

Sallie Gardner running at Palo Alto, 1878. The bottom right photo, showing the horse at rest, was evidently taken separately from the others. Frame number three shows all the galloping horse's hooves off the ground and gathered beneath its body.

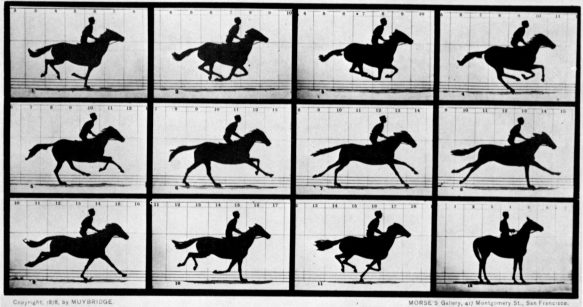

Copyright, 1878, by MUYBRIDGE.

MORSE'S Gallery, 417 Montgomery St., San Francisco.

THE HORSE IN MOTION.
Illustrated by
MUYBRIDGE.
AUTOMATIC ELECTRO-PHOTOGRAPH.
"SALLIE GARDNER," owned by LELAND STANFORD; running at a 1.40 gait over the Palo Alto track, 19th June, 1878.
The negatives of these photographs were made at intervals of twenty-seven inches of distance, and about the twenty-fifth part of a second of time; they illustrate consecutive positions assumed in each twenty-seven inches of progress during a single stride of the mare. The vertical lines were twenty-seven inches apart; the horizontal lines represent elevations of four inches each. The exposure of each negative was less than the two-thousandth part of a second.

In the fall, engravings from his first photo series were published in America and Europe. Throughout the world the pictures were hailed as a revelation. For the first time, scientists had accurate representations of animal movement, facts instead of guesses. Horse fanciers found many of their misconceptions totally shattered. Artists realized how unnatural many of their depictions of motion had been.

Étienne Marey (ay-TYEN ma-RAY), a French scientist who had performed early experiments in animal locomotion, wrote, "I am lost with admiration of these photographs," and asked Muybridge to train his cameras on flying birds. Obsessed with realism in his paintings, artist Thomas Eakins (AY-kinz) used Muybridge's motion studies to help him portray moving horses on canvas.

So gratifying was all this praise that Stanford and Muybridge expanded their project still further. They added twelve more cameras to the original dozen so that motions could be analyzed in greater detail. Muybridge developed a way to photograph a single movement from five different angles at once. And since his original methods could capture only regular movement in a straight line, he designed a clockwork mechanism to fire his shutters automatically. With it he could photograph a far greater variety of subjects.

A picture Muybridge often used for comic effect in his lectures. He considered the horses' postures totally unrealistic.

34

A back somersault. One of the later Palo Alto series, taken with a clockwork device to trip the shutters. From *The Attitudes of Animals in Motion*, 1881.

Dogs, deer, cows, oxen, an uncooperative boar, a frisky goat, and the birds Marey had requested went before the cameras and had their patterns of movement analyzed for the very first time. With his clockwork device, Muybridge photographed human athletes boxing, wrestling, fencing, and tumbling. Not to be outdone, he sprinted past the cameras himself.

In 1881, Muybridge published the results of his work in a beautiful album called *The Attitudes of Animals in Motion*. Stanford had sunk more than forty thousand dollars into the project, but rather than complain about the cost, he bragged about it. He had gotten his money's worth, for now he could develop a theory of locomotion—the topic that had intrigued him for so long.

And Muybridge, who had patented his "Method and Apparatus for Photographing Objects in Motion," rarely bothered taking pictures of landscapes and still subjects anymore. The idea of motion captivated him, and he was only just beginning to explore it.

35

# 5. THE AMAZING ZOOPRAXISCOPE

Now that he had separated motions into individual parts, Eadweard Muybridge wondered whether he might be able to put the parts back together again and somehow re-create the motions he had captured. He thought of various toys that demonstrated the principle of "persistence of vision"—the fact that when the eye sees a series of still pictures in quick enough succession, the brain tends to link them together in an illusion of continuous movement.

With the zoetrope (ZOE-uh-trope), for example, you merely had to put a special strip of pictures into a slotted drum and give the drum a spin. If you looked through the slots, the pictures would magically appear to move. A girl would jump rope over and over, or a boy would endlessly toss a ball in the air and catch it. Of course, the pictures for such devices had always been drawn, painted, or photographically posed to simu-

36

A disc used to project motion pictures in the zoopraxiscope. The images appear "stretched out" on the disc so that they will look correct when projected onto the screen.

late motion. Before Muybridge, no one had ever taken sequential photos of real movement.

When the magazine *Scientific American* published Muybridge's horse studies, the editor suggested that they might work perfectly in a zoetrope. Muybridge quickly tested his pictures in one of these toys and found the editor was right. But only a few people at a time could use a zoetrope, and its images were small. Muybridge wanted to reconstruct motion in a more lifelike size before the large audiences that were flocking to his lectures.

Using principles of the zoetrope and similar devices, Muybridge built a special machine. From a spinning glass disc of pictures taken from his motion studies, it could project realistic moving images on a screen. With his fondness for unusual names—and in keeping with a long tradition of giving motion    37

Muybridge's zoopraxiscope. The box on legs at the right is the light source. The disc immediately to the left (and partially obscured) carries the images of movement (see illustration on page 37).
To turn the disc, the projectionist cranks the wheel at upper left. The light shines through the spinning disc and the lens at top left to project an image onto a screen.

picture devices jawbreaking Greek labels—he dubbed his invention the zoopraxiscope (zoe-uh-PRAKS-uh-skope). The name combined the Greek words for "animal," "action," and "to look."

Muybridge set up his machine at a private party at Stanford's Palo Alto mansion in the fall of 1879. When he dimmed the gaslights, the guests expected to see lantern slides of his latest photographs. To their astonishment, what turned up on the screen was a likeness of a horse that appeared to be running right before their eyes!

38

"There, Governor," said Muybridge calmly, as the image continued to run in place, "you have a representation of Hawthorn galloping at a one-forty-two gait."

"I think you must make a mistake in the name of the animal," Leland Stanford replied without missing a beat. "That is certainly not the gait of Hawthorn but of Anderson."

Muybridge leafed through his notes. According to his records, the moving image was definitely of Hawthorn. Stanford remained unconvinced. He sent for his horse trainer.

The trainer was sheepish. Muybridge was supposed to have photographed Hawthorn at that particular session, he admitted. But he had substituted Anderson and forgotten to mention it.

The Governor smiled and puffed up with conceit; no one knew horses the way he did. After cursing his faulty records, Muybridge smiled inwardly himself, for he now knew just how convincing his zoopraxiscope pictures could be. And Anderson might have felt proud too, had anyone realized that she was the world's first "movie star." That evening, Eadweard Muybridge had become the first person ever to project moving pictures from photographs of real movement. For more than ten years, he remained the only one in the world who could do it.

Muybridge gave the first public demonstration of his new invention before the San Francisco Art Association on May 4, 1880. "Nothing was wanting but the clatter of hoofs upon the turf and an occasional breath of steam to make the spectator believe he had before him the flesh and blood steeds," declared one newspaper the next day.

"Horses of life size were represented running, trotting, and jumping; men, deer, bulls, and dogs ran with all the motions of life," reported another. "Mr. Muybridge has laid the foundations of a new method of educating the people, and we predict that his instantaneous, photographic, magic-lantern zoetrope will make the rounds of the civilized world." In a curious way, that prediction soon came true.

Like Thomas Eakins, the French artist Jean Louis Ernest Meissonier (may-sun-YAY) tried to make his paintings as true  39 to life as possible. Horses were one of his great passions, and he studied them tirelessly. At his country home, Meissonier had built a small railway just so he could ride alongside horses and observe their movements. In studying the gallop, he had worked one of his horses so hard that the poor animal had broken down. Yet he still wasn't satisfied. When he discovered a few of Muybridge's astonishing photos in a French journal, he hungered to see more.

Not long afterward, a rich American visitor asked Meissonier to paint his portrait. The temperamental artist refused; he had better things to paint than well-fed foreign millionaires. Then the American mentioned some horse photographs he had commissioned.

Meissonier's eyes lit up. "Are these the pictures I have seen in the magazines?"

"Yes," replied Leland Stanford, "and hundreds more besides."

Meissonier extended his hand. "I will paint your portrait," he declared, "if you will show me your photographs."

The bargain was sealed. Muybridge's pictures delighted Meissonier so much that he painted the Governor's album of them into his portrait. And during the sittings, the Frenchman convinced Stanford to bring Eadweard Muybridge to Europe.

Back home, Muybridge's talks were going well. The moving pictures he used to illustrate them were so convincing that at one lecture someone's dog chased the phantom horses on the screen. Muybridge had become something of a celebrity around San Francisco, but he could not have begun to imagine the kind of reception that awaited him abroad.

In September 1881 Muybridge arrived in Paris to a hero's welcome. Étienne Marey, now working on photographic motion studies of his own, greeted him warmly. Muybridge displayed his photos and his astounding zoopraxiscope at a gala reception, and Marey acted as translator. At another great gathering, Meissonier introduced Muybridge to the artistic community, declaring that his photographs opened new worlds to
40 them.

Leland Stanford as portrayed by J. L. E. Meissonier. A copy of *The Attitudes of Animals in Motion* is visible beneath Stanford's left arm.

Muybridge lecturing before The Royal Society in London.
An 1889 magazine cover.

Muybridge lectured before the most prestigious institutions of the city, but he most enjoyed his conversations with the like-minded Marey. Marey showed Muybridge his new invention, a "photographic gun" that could take repeated exposures on a single plate. More importantly, he introduced Muybridge to the new gelatin dry-plate process of taking pictures. The new plates were more detailed and more sensitive than the old ones. Better still, they were more manageable, since they could be prepared in advance and developed at the photographer's convenience. Like most who tried this new method, Muybridge never again went back to the old one.

Muybridge's tour of his native England began as successfully as his visit to France. Although he was not presented to Queen Victoria, he did give a demonstration of his work to an enthusiastic audience that included the Prince of Wales, the Duke of Edinburgh, the Prime Minister, and the Poet Laureate. He spoke before the Royal Academy and the Royal Institution, and he began planning a new series of motion studies even more ambitious than the last.

Then he received a copy of *The Horse in Motion*, a book Leland Stanford had just published. It was the study of horses' movements that the Governor long had dreamed of. The doctor Stanford had hired to write it had based most of his conclusions on Muybridge's work. But to Muybridge's great dismay, his photographs were drastically altered in the book, represented by poor drawings that didn't even copy his work correctly. Worse, his role in the studies was barely mentioned; his name did not even appear on the title page. Muybridge was deeply wounded, and he let Stanford know it. Stanford considered Muybridge ungrateful. Their relationship came to an abrupt end.

And the rift dealt Muybridge's career a brutal blow. The Royal Society of London had invited him to publish a paper based on his work, and had offered to finance him in further investigations. But when *The Horse in Motion* appeared under someone else's name, the Society retracted its offer until Muybridge could prove that he had actually done the original research. Only Leland Stanford could help him provide that

43

THE

# HORSE IN MOTION

AS SHOWN BY INSTANTANEOUS PHOTOGRAPHY

## WITH A STUDY ON ANIMAL MECHANICS

FOUNDED ON ANATOMY AND THE REVELATIONS
OF THE CAMERA

*IN WHICH IS DEMONSTRATED THE THEORY OF QUADRUPEDAL LOCOMOTION*

By J. D. B. STILLMAN, A.M., M.D.

———

EXECUTED AND PUBLISHED UNDER THE AUSPICES OF

## LELAND STANFORD

BOSTON
JAMES R. OSGOOD AND COMPANY
1882

The title page of *The Horse in Motion*. Muybridge's name does not appear anywhere, even though the book is based primarily on his work.

proof, and the Governor refused to do so. Bitter, Muybridge returned to the United States and sued Stanford for using his copyrighted photographs without permission.

Three years later, Muybridge lost the suit. But by then the matter no longer meant as much to him. He had finally found support for a new project, and he was already deeply involved in carrying it out.

# 6. ANIMAL LOCOMOTION

Sometimes scientific discovery requires nothing more than a good brain. Sometimes it also requires a good deal of money. Without a patron, Muybridge could not hope to begin the new work he wanted so badly to do. He planned a comprehensive study of "The Attitudes of Man, the Horse, and other Animals in Motion," with emphasis on humans, but he needed to find funds for the expensive equipment the project would require. To support himself in the meantime, he kept on giving his illustrated lectures. He hoped some of his wealthier, more imaginative listeners might decide to back him.

In 1884, through the efforts of Philadelphia artist Thomas Eakins and his patron Fairman Rogers, both amateur photographers, Muybridge finally found the financing he needed. A committee of six prominent Philadelphians agreed to advance five thousand dollars each, to be repaid from the sale of Muy-

Hornet, a chestnut horse, jumping over three other horses. Later pictures in the same series show that Hornet's leap was successful. From *Animal Locomotion*, 1886.

bridge's new photographs. The University of Pennsylvania offered facilities for the experiments and appointed a faculty committee to advise him.

Muybridge accepted these arrangements with gratitude and pride. At last he would be behind his cameras again! And even though it was not an official title, the man who had never gone beyond grammar school was tickled to hear himself called "Professor."

In Philadelphia Muybridge developed new equipment far more versatile than any he had used before. The clockwork mechanism that controlled his new electric shutters also created a graph showing the precise interval between each picture. In addition to a fixed set of twenty-four cameras, he now had two portable sets—batteries, as he called them—of twelve cameras each. With these he could take pictures away from the studio. 47

Or he could connect them to the fixed set and shoot sequential views from three angles at once. The sensitive new dry plates allowed him to make each exposure more rapidly than before and get sharper, more detailed pictures. And no longer did he have to waste precious daylight sensitizing and developing his plates immediately before and after exposure.

With his new equipment, Muybridge was prepared to explore the movement of humans in every action imaginable. Before his cameras, people walked, ran, jumped, turned, climbed, crawled, hopped, stooped, danced, sat, rose, kneeled, dressed, undressed, ironed, washed, drank, and curtseyed. Athletes demonstrated the motions of baseball, football, tennis,

"Charging bayonet." A typical plate, much reduced, from the University of Pennsylvania series, *Animal Locomotion*, 1887. The three rows of pictures were taken at the same time by Muybridge's three electrically-connected "batteries" of twelve cameras. The missing portions of the pictures in the top row, center, are due to defective original negatives—a problem that plagued Muybridge continually.

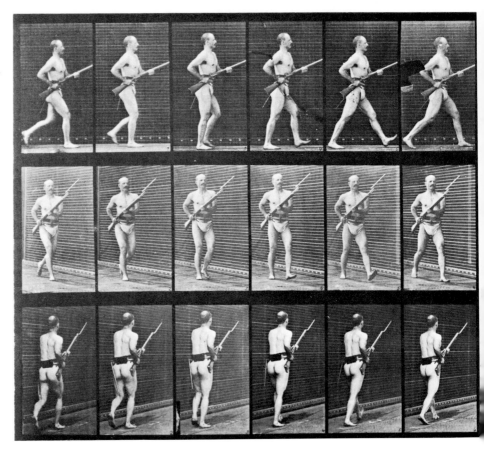

48

cricket, boxing, wrestling, fencing, shot-putting, discus throwing, weight lifting, rowing, and tumbling. A soldier drilled with a bayonet. Workmen shod horses, planed boards, laid bricks, sowed seeds, and mowed grass as three dozen cameras captured their movements. And in one humorous series, which Muybridge later called "A Shock to the Nervous System," one woman poured cold water over another.

Because the action of muscles was so important in these studies, Muybridge asked many of his models to appear nude before the cameras. A few times he even did so himself. But even though a tall fence had been erected around the studio to insure privacy, Muybridge occasionally failed to persuade mod-

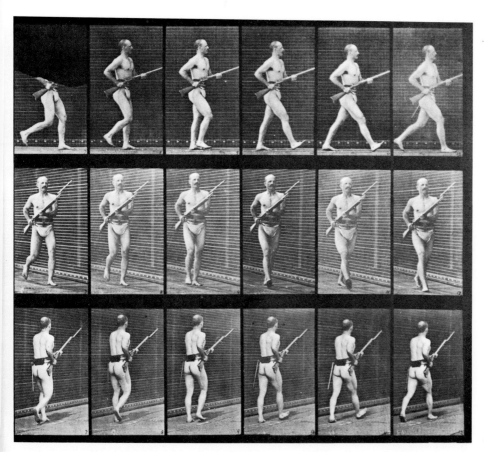

49

"Boxing." As in the illustrations on pp. 48–49 and p. 51, the background is divided by threads into squares 5 centimeters (about 2 inches) wide. From *Animal Locomotion*, 1887.

est bricklayers and carpenters to shed their clothes in the interest of science.

Animals could be stubborner still. At the Philadelphia Zoo, one pigeon absolutely refused to budge from its cage. Coaxed out at last, it flew straight up, completely avoiding the cameras. When Muybridge's assistants carefully lowered a portable backdrop into the lions' den, the curious animals clawed it to shreds. The zoo's donkey stopped just before coming into camera range, then cavorted across the lawn for half an hour until he was captured. A cat ran under the snake house and refused to come out.

Despite these difficulties, Muybridge and his assistants succeeded more often than not. In addition to numerous birds, they photographed mule, ass, ox, sow, goat, oryx, deer, elk, eland, antelope, giraffe, buffalo, gnu, dog, lion, jaguar, elephant, camel, guanaco, raccoon, capybara, baboon, sloth, and kangaroo.

The work absorbed Muybridge almost totally, and he neglected nearly everything else. Colleagues at the University commented on the way his bushy gray hair stuck out through the holes in his hat. His trousers were woefully threadbare, and his long beard was streaked with stains from his cheap cigars. Muybridge didn't seem to notice. Who had time to buy new hats and pants when he was discovering things no human eye had ever seen?

For the benefit of doctors, Muybridge captured the abnormal walks of patients with diseases and disabilities. Modifying his equipment, he photographed the beating hearts of a dog and a turtle whose bodies had been opened surgically. Rarely before had the camera been used to serve the medical profession.

Late in 1887, Muybridge published the results of his efforts. *Animal Locomotion* was a massive work. Its 781 huge pages contained more than twenty thousand individual photographs. For the first time, ornithologists could learn how fast a flying bird flaps its wings, and see the way its feathers turn and separate in flight. Zoologists could compare the strides of various animals. Artists and physicians could study the action of human muscles in an overwhelming variety of situations.

The work received glowing reviews, but its unwieldy size

"Walking, flirting a fan." This plate is much reduced, as are the illustrations on pp. 48–49 and p. 50. The originals were printed on paper nineteen inches high and two feet wide. The woman's motion took place over approximately one and a half seconds. From *Animal Locomotion,* 1887.

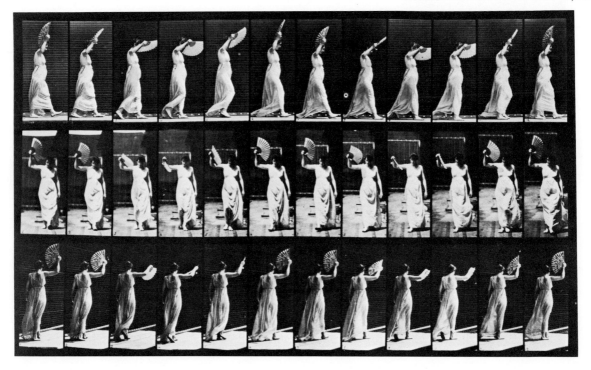

and high price made it difficult to sell. Feeling obligated to help his backers recover their investment, Muybridge embarked on lecture tours of the United States and Europe. By showing slides and zoopraxiscope pictures based on his latest work, he hoped to drum up sales for it.

The list of purchasers eventually included many of the world's scientific and artistic institutions, as well as prominent artists and scientists, former United States President Rutherford B. Hayes, and inventor Thomas Edison. But although audiences everywhere received Muybridge's lectures enthusiastically, *Animal Locomotion*, much to his disappointment, failed to earn back its cost.

In 1893, Muybridge was invited to participate in the World's Columbian Exposition. He accepted at once. This world's fair in Chicago might be the perfect place to find a wider audience for his work. He might sell more copies of *Animal Locomotion*, and he might even find a backer for his latest plan, a study of the flight of insects. But competing against the fair's other attractions, his "Zoopraxographical Hall" drew far fewer customers than he'd hoped. Fairgoers preferred to gawk at the scandalous belly dancer "Little Egypt" or ride the world's first Ferris wheel.

Perhaps they simply couldn't guess what was inside the building with the unpronounceable name. Nevertheless, people were still as fascinated as ever with the wonders of motion. When Muybridge began a new lecture tour after the fair, he met with his usual success.

Then Thomas Edison introduced a new machine he called the Kinetoscope (kuh-NET-uh-skope). For a nickel, the customer could peer through its little window and see moving pictures. Taken on celluloid film instead of plates, using one camera instead of many, Edison's pictures were far more detailed and realistic than Muybridge's. And though the Kinetoscope pictures flashed before the viewer for less than a minute each, at least they didn't repeat themselves every few seconds the way zoopraxiscope pictures did. Within a year, pictures like Edison's had been projected on a screen. Soon "movies," as

52

Zoopraxigraphical Hall at the World's Columbian Exposition, Chicago, 1893. Muybridge exhibited his still and moving pictures here. The height and depth of the building are exaggerated in this picture. From *Descriptive Zoopraxography*, 1893.

people nicknamed them, became a mania. Edison's basic method had won out. It's still in use for movies today.

In 1896, Muybridge returned to his birthplace in England, where he completed two books reprinting many of his motion studies and summing up everything he had learned about human and animal locomotion. He never claimed to be the inventor of the motion picture, but he rightly declared that he had invented the first instrument for reconstructing "movements originally photographed from life."

Retired from photography, Eadweard Muybridge lived to see the day when motion pictures would capture the imagination of the world. In 1904, at the time of his death in Kingston-on-Thames, he was digging ground in his garden to build a model of the Great Lakes of the United States—the country where he had done his greatest work.

That work lives on in every motion picture we see today, and in every photograph of rapid action. Each one has its roots in the experiments that began with a millionaire's questions about his racehorses, and Eadweard Muybridge's ability to provide the answers.

Eadweard Muybridge in 1893. From *Descriptive Zoopraxography*.

# BIBLIOGRAPHY

Clark, George T. *Leland Stanford: War Governor of California, Railroad Builder, and Founder of Stanford University.* Palo Alto: Stanford University Press, 1931.

Gréard, Vallery C. O. *Meissonier: His Life and Art.* Translated by Mary Loyd and Florance Simmonds. London: William Heinemann, 1897.

Haas, Robert Bartlett. *Muybridge: Man in Motion.* Berkeley: University of California Press, 1976.

Hendricks, Gordon. *Eadweard Muybridge: The Father of the Motion Picture.* New York: Grossman Publishers, 1975.

Lewis, Oscar. *The Big Four: The Story of Huntington, Stanford, Hopkins, Crocker, and of the Building of the Central Pacific.* New York: Alfred A. Knopf, 1938.

——— *San Francisco: Mission to Metropolis.* Berkeley: Howell-North, 1966.

MacDonnell, Kevin. *Eadweard Muybridge: The Man Who Invented the Moving Picture.* Boston: Little, Brown, 1972.

55

Muybridge, Eadweard. *Animal Locomotion: An Electro-Photographic Investigation of Consecutive Phases of Animal Movement.* Philadelphia: University of Pennsylvania, 1887.

———— *Animals in Motion.* London: Chapman and Hall, 1899.

———— *The Attitudes of Animals in Motion.* San Francisco: 1881.

———— *Descriptive Zoopraxography, or the Science of Animal Locomotion Made Popular.* Chicago: University of Pennsylvania (?), 1893.

———— *The Human Figure in Motion.* London: Chapman and Hall, 1901.

Newhall, Beaumont. *The History of Photography.* New York: Museum of Modern Art, 1964.

Stanford University, Department of Art. *Eadweard Muybridge: The Stanford Years, 1872–1882.* Palo Alto: Stanford University, 1974.

Stillman, J.D.B. *The Horse in Motion.* Boston: James Osgood and Co., 1882.

The following reprint, far easier to find than Muybridge's original works cited above, contains all the Philadelphia motion studies:

Muybridge, Eadweard. *Muybridge's Complete Human and Animal Locomotion.* Three volumes. New York: Dover, Inc., 1979.

# INDEX